NAILED IT!

Extreme MOUNTAIN CLIMBING

Virginia Loh-Hagan

45th Parallel Press

Published in the United States of America by Cherry Lake Publishing
Ann Arbor, Michigan
www.cherrylakepublishing.com

Content Adviser: Liv Williams, Editor, www.iLivExtreme.com
Reading Adviser: Marla Conn, ReadAbility, Inc.
Photo Credits: ©My Good Images/Shutterstock.com, cover, 1; ©deamles for sale/Shutterstock.com, 5; ©Sirizhatr Karrassamee/Shutterstock.com, 6; ©Stefan Petrovski/Shutterstock.com, 8; ©Iuliia Kryzhevska/Dreamstime.com, 11; ©Yongyut Kumsri/Shutterstock.com, 13; ©Evgeniya Moroz/Shutterstock.com, 15; ©Mostovyi Sergii Igorevich/Shutterstock.com, 17; ©bikeriderlondon/Shutterstock.com, 19; ©Images & Stories/Alamy Stock, 21; ©Christianmalos/Dreamstime.com, 23; ©Peter Montgomery/Dreamstime.com, 25; ©mountainpix/Shutterstock.com, 27; ©JoyfulThailand/Thinkstock.com, 28; ©Trusjom/Shutterstock.com, multiple interior pages; ©Kues/Shutterstock.com, multiple interior pages

45th Parallel Press is an imprint of Cherry Lake Publishing.

Library of Congress Cataloging-in-Publication Data

Loh-Hagan, Virginia.
Extreme mountain climbing / by Virginia Loh-Hagan.
pages cm. -- (Nailed it!)
Includes bibliographical references and index.
ISBN 978-1-63470-491-5 (hardcover) -- ISBN 978-1-63470-551-6 (pdf) -- ISBN 978-1-63470-611-7 (paperback) -- ISBN 978-1-63470-671-1 (ebook)
1. Mountaineering--Juvenile literature. 2. Extreme sports--Juvenile literature. I. Title.
GV200.L675 2016
796.522--dc23
2015026875

ABOUT THE AUTHOR

Dr. Virginia Loh-Hagan is an author, university professor, former classroom teacher, and curriculum designer. She likes driving up mountains to see the view. She lives in San Diego with her very tall husband and very naughty dogs. To learn more about her, visit www.virginialoh.com.

Table of Contents

About the Author 2

CHAPTER 1:
At the Top of the World 4

CHAPTER 2:
Climbers and Mountains 10

CHAPTER 3:
Going Extreme. 14

CHAPTER 4:
First without Oxygen 20

CHAPTER 5:
Dangers on the Mountain 24

Did You Know? 30

Consider This! 31

Learn More 31

Glossary 32

Index 32

1

At the Top of the World

Who is Gerlinde Kaltenbrunner? Who is Edmund Viesturs? Who is Kim Chang-ho? What is the significance of "14 eight-thousanders"?

Gerlinde Kaltenbrunner slowly climbed up. The snow was deep. The air was thin. The winds were rough. She couldn't feel her fingers and toes. She climbed up steep slopes. She strained her legs. She finally **summited** the mountain. To summit means to reach the top.

She tried to climb K2 six times. It's the second-highest mountain in the world. One time, she saw a climber fall. He died. Another time, the weather was too cold.

She became the second woman to climb the 14 **eight-thousanders**. Eight-thousanders means mountains that are over 8,000 meters tall. That's 26,247 feet. There are 14 of them. They're in the Himalayan mountain range. They're in central Asia.

She's the first woman to do so without using oxygen tanks. She did it without **porters**. Porters carry people's gear.

Eight-thousanders are the tallest mountains in the world.

Edmund Viesturs climbed up. He took a step. He breathed 18 times. He gasped for air. He took another step.

He summited Annapurna. It has the highest climber death rate. It has no clear route to the top. There are falling rocks. He tried two other times. He said, "The art of mountaineering is knowing when to go, when to stay, and when to retreat."

He became the first American to climb the 14 eight-thousanders. He's the fifth person to do so without oxygen tanks. He thinks bringing oxygen is cheating. He said, "It brings the mountain down to your level. … If I have to train harder or suffer more, then so be it. And if I can't get

NAILED IT!

Advice from the Field: Malavath Poorna

Malavath Poorna is the youngest girl to summit Mount Everest. She was 13 years and 11 months old. She's from India. She's from a poor family. Her parents are farm workers. She wanted to prove that anyone could do anything. She dealt with the cold and the climb. She climbed with an experienced mountaineer, her friend, and a group of sherpas. She was challenged by the packaged food. She said, "I did not like its smell or taste." She wanted to eat her mother's food. Bodies of dead climbers also scared her. She said, "I saw six dead bodies." But she remained brave. She advised herself to think good thoughts. She thought about her parents. Her good thoughts paid off. She said, "When I reached the top, I felt too much emotion, too much joy."

Mountain climbers face many challenges.

to the top without oxygen, then I'll never get to the top."

Kim Chang-ho started at sea level. He canoed up a river. He biked. Then he climbed. He summited Everest. It's the world's highest mountain. It's 29,029 feet (8,848 m) tall. He became the first Korean to climb the 14 eight-thousanders without oxygen tanks. He did it without porters. He set a world record. He did it in the shortest time span. It took him seven years, 10 months, and six days.

Coming down, a fellow climber died. Chang-ho was lonely. He imagined a friend. He ran out of food. He battled the weather. But Chang-ho said, "On the top of mountains, I feel a great sense of accomplishment. And this is indeed the most rewarding moment."

"And if I can't get to the top without oxygen, then I'll never get to the top."

2

Climbers and Mountains

What are some skills mountain climbers need? Who is Jordan Romero? What are the Seven Summits? What gear do mountain climbers need?

Mountain climbers put their hands and feet on rock, ice, and snow. They deal with harsh weather. They deal with nature. They climb steep slopes. Their goal is to summit.

Jordan Romero is the youngest person to climb Everest. He was 13 years and 10 months old. He's also the youngest person to climb the Seven Summits. The Seven Summits are the highest mountains of each continent. His goal was "to stand on top of the world." A poster inspired him. It was in his school hallway. The poster was of the Seven Summits.

Mountain climbers break up their climbs. They climb a segment. They camp. They climb the next segment.

Mountain climbers wear special clothes. The clothes must resist wind and water. Climbers need jackets, hats, and masks. They need socks. They need boots. Some boots have heating pads. They need gloves.

Mountain climbers must adjust to mountain air.

NAILED IT!

Spotlight Biography: Ivan Vallejo

Ivan Vallejo is from Ecuador. He was a chemical engineer. He quit his job. He followed his passion for mountains. He dreamed about being a mountain climber at age seven. He admired the cone shape of a nearby volcano. At age 12, he drew a picture of a mountaineer on top of Everest. He's climbed many mountains. His main goal was to summit all 14 eight-thousanders without oxygen. He did this in 2008. He was the first Ecuadorian to do so. He said, "There are always challenges, things you've never done before and you'd like to try." He likes snow adventures. He likes figuring out obstacles. He started a climbing team from Ecuador. They want to summit Everest without oxygen. They want to do it as a team. He also started a campaign to help survivors of the 2015 Nepal earthquake.

Mountain climbers need special gear. They use ropes and other climbing gear. They use **crampons**. Crampons are attached to boots. They clamp on to the ice and snow.

They use an ice ax. An ice ax carves steps. It anchors climbers. It stops falls.

Mountain climbers climb. But they also camp. They need sleeping bags. They need tents. They need cooking supplies. They need bottles for water. Most also need oxygen tanks.

Many mountain climbers hire porters to carry their things.

3

Going Extreme

How do mountain climbers make mountain climbing extreme? What happens at the "death zone"? Who is Laval St. Germain?

For some, climbing mountains is not enough. Extreme mountain climbers create more challenges. They climb the world's most dangerous peaks. They climb the world's highest peaks. They climb mountains in record time. They don't use mountain guides. They don't use porters. The most extreme is climbing without oxygen.

Mountain climbing is a high-**altitude** sport. It takes place high above ground. The air pressure is lower. The weather is colder. There's less oxygen. Humans need oxygen to breathe.

Humans can't live above 26,000 feet (7,925 m). It's called the death zone. There's not enough oxygen. The body uses oxygen faster than it can be replaced. So climbers **suffocate**. They can't breathe.

When climbers reach the death zone, they have to summit in two or three days. Climbers take 12 hours to hike 1 mile (1.6 kilometers). Even eating takes a lot of energy.

Other high-altitude sports include skiing, snowboarding, and BASE jumping.

The human body tires easily.

Extreme mountain climbers fully experience the mountain. They climb higher. And their bodies work harder.

Mountain climbers have to get used to high altitudes. They need time to adjust to mountain air. That's why climbers camp. That's why they train in high altitudes. They practice climbing many mountains. They learn rock- and ice-climbing skills. They study weather.

Laval St. Germain said, "I'm always training. I ride my bike to work all the time. I go to the gym every day. I do **ultra marathons**." Ultra marathons are more than 26 miles (42 km).

He summited Everest. He did it without oxygen tanks. He was the first Canadian to do so. He said, "I didn't take oxygen with me. … I thought that climbing the highest mountain in the world with oxygen is somehow—I don't

Mountain climbers try to save their energy when they are high in the mountains.

NAILED IT!

When Extreme Is Too Extreme!

A group of daredevil mountain climbers performed several death-defying stunts. They were 13,641 feet (4,158 m) high. They were in the Swiss mountains. They did it for an outdoor clothing company. They honored the 1865 first ascent of the Matterhorn. They celebrated its 150th anniversary. In one stunt, there was a chain of red lights on the route. The mountain lit up. The daredevils did nighttime ski jumps. They climbed steep rock faces together. In another stunt, the daredevils climbed up 98 feet (30 m). Each daredevil climbed a vertically hanging rope. They waited for each daredevil to get in a straight line. They waited for two hours. They created a horizontal line in the air. In yet another stunt, the daredevils made an X. They made it with their bodies. They were on steep slopes. X stands for extreme.

want to say cheating. But it's not the pure way to do it. I thought if you couldn't climb a peak without oxygen, then maybe you shouldn't be up there."

Climbing and camping in the death zone is dangerous.

4

First Without Oxygen

What did Reinhold Messner and Peter Habeler do?
Why are they important to the sport of mountain climbing?

For a long time, people thought summiting tall mountains without oxygen tanks would be impossible. Reinhold Messner and Peter Habeler did the impossible. They climbed without oxygen tanks. People thought they were crazy.

In 1975, they climbed Hidden Peak. It's in the Himalayas. It's 26,470 feet (8,068 m) tall. They didn't use porters, camps, fixed ropes, or oxygen. Messner said he would only do it "by fair means." Or he wouldn't do it at all. It took three days. They introduced extreme mountain climbing.

In 1978, Messner and Habeler climbed Everest. They didn't use oxygen tanks. This wasn't their first try. On a previous try, Habeler got sick. He ate a bad can of sardines. They were trapped in a storm. They turned back.

They gasped for air. They got headaches. Messner said, "Breathing becomes such a **strenuous** business that we scarcely have strength left to go on. Every 10 or 15 steps, we collapse into the snow to rest. Then, crawl on again." Strenuous means difficult.

Mountain climbers risk frostbite. Frostbite is when body parts get frozen.

Extreme Mountain Climbing: Know the Lingo

Alpine start: starting in the early morning

Ascent: climbing up the mountain

Assault team: two or more climbers who try to reach a mountain summit

Behemoth: very large mountain

Col: a low spot or pass in a mountain range

Cornice: an overhanging mass of hard snow at the edge of a ridge

Crevasse: a deep, open crack in a glacier

Cwm: a valley on the side of a hill or mountain

Deck: the ground

Descent: climbing down the mountain

Dinnerplating: shattering of hard ice that can occur when a climber strikes the mountain with an ice ax

Gripped: scared

Icefall: a cascade of ice from a glacier coming down a slope

Sherpa: porter, mountain guide

Traverse: to cross a mountain slope

Wand: a bamboo stick with a small flag on top to mark paths

Talking takes a lot of energy. Mountain climbers will use hand signals instead of talking.

In 1980, Messner climbed Everest alone. He was the first to do so. He did it without oxygen. He only had a small backpack. He was the first to climb 14 eight-thousanders.

5

Dangers on the Mountain

What are some dangers mountain climbers face?

Mountains are filled with danger. Lightning can strike. Storms form quickly. Rocks fall. **Avalanches** happen. Avalanches are quick flows of snow down a slope.

Nepal is a country. It's close to Everest. There was an earthquake. The earthquake started an avalanche. The avalanche hit a **base camp**. A base camp is where climbers and helpers prepare for climbs. It's where tents, food, gear, and medical supplies are stored.

Seventeen people died. Sixty-one people were injured. Ada Tsang is a climber. She said, "I thought I was dreaming."

She was knocked out. She got cuts on her head. Five people from her group died. About 180 climbers were stuck above base camp.

Accidents happen. Climbers fall. Climbers get trapped. Climbers get hurt. Climbers die. One in ten climbers dies trying to climb up Everest. One in twenty dies coming down.

Base camp is an important place for mountain climbers to rest.

Chris Bonington and Doug Scott were the first to summit "The **Ogre**." Ogre means monster. It's a rock and ice tower. It's 23,901 feet (7,285 m) tall. It's in Pakistan.

They got hurt coming down. Scott slipped on ice. He hit a rock wall. He broke both his legs. He crawled. They found a cave. A storm hit. They stayed in the cave for two nights. Then Bonington fell. He broke two ribs. They made it to base camp. They waited several days. They were finally rescued.

Climbing without oxygen is dangerous. Mountain climbers freeze easily. The body directs blood to the chest and brain. Climbers often lose fingers and toes. They get sick easily. They get chest pains. Their mind plays tricks on them. They can damage their brains. Their lungs can fill with **fluid**. Fluid is like water.

Lincoln Hall summited Everest. Coming down, his brain swelled. He got really tired. He saw things that weren't there. People tried to help him. But their supplies were low.

Experts don't consider an attempt successful if climbers don't make it down the mountain on their own.

Mountain climbers can get several types of altitude sicknesses.

They had to leave him. People thought he'd die. But he lived. He didn't have oxygen. He didn't have gear. He was rescued. He lost a toe. He lost the tips of eight fingers.

Climbers risk a lot to be on top!

"People tried to help him. But their supplies were low."

NAILED IT!

That Happened?!?

There are more than 200 corpses on Everest. Corpses are bodies of people who died. Bodies are preserved by the extreme sun, snow, and ice. Climbers pass the frozen dead bodies. Some bodies become landmarks. "Green Boots" was an Indian climber. He wore bright green boots. There was a blizzard. He got separated from his group. He died in 1996. He's near a cave. The cave is called Green Boots' Cave. All climbers must pass it. Climbers use him as a marker. They use him to see how close they are to the summit. The cave is 27,890 feet (8,501 m) high. People throw away used oxygen tanks there. Guide services have climbers sign a form. It's called a body disposal form. Climbers decide what to do with their bodies if they die. They can leave their bodies behind. Or they can have their bodies recovered. This can cost over $30,000.

Did You Know?

- Sherpas live in the Himalayas. They carry things for mountain climbers. Sherpas have adapted to mountain air. They live in high altitudes. They live with low oxygen. Sherpas hold many records. They have done the most summits. They have done the quickest climbs up. They have done the quickest climbs down. They have spent the most time on top.
- Velvet is a black dog. She saved three mountain climbers. The climbers were trapped in a storm. They were on Mount Hood. They had to spend the night. Velvet slept over them. She went from person to person. She kept them warm. Dogs are warmer than humans. They were all rescued the next morning.
- Barbara Washburn was the first woman to climb Mount McKinley. This is the United States' highest peak. She climbed it in 1947.
- The tallest known mountain in the solar system is Olympus Mons. It's on Mars.
- The Yeti is a manlike animal. It's mythical. It's believed to live mostly in the Himalayas. It's over 6 feet (183 centimeters) tall. It weighs 200 to 400 pounds (91 to 181 kilograms). It's hairy. It makes a whistling sound. It smells bad. It throws stones at humans.
- Yaks are cowlike animals. They live in the Himalayas. They're used to carrying things. Their poop, or dung, is used as cooking fuel.

Consider This!

TAKE A POSITION! Reread chapter one. Pay close attention to what Edmund Viesturs said about using oxygen. Do you think using oxygen while mountain climbing is cheating? Argue your point with reasons and evidence.

SAY WHAT? Mountain climbing without oxygen is dangerous. Explain why it's dangerous. Explain how lack of oxygen affects mountain climbers.

THINK ABOUT IT! Mountain climbers leave trash on the mountain. Trash includes human poop. Rangers haul out over a ton of trash several times a year. This is one of the reasons why Reinhold Messner climbs with little help. He limits what he carries to the mountain. He doesn't bring oxygen tanks. Climbers toss their empty tanks on the mountain paths. What do you think about the trash problem?

SEE A DIFFERENT SIDE! Some people think it's irresponsible to not use oxygen. They think mountain climbers should be fit to function. They think climbers should be able to help others. What do you think about this perspective? Can you see their point of view?

Learn More: Resources

PRIMARY SOURCES

Cold, a documentary about climbing mountains in Pakistan (Forge Motion Pictures, 2011).

Romero, Jordan, with Linda LeBlanc. *No Summit Out of Sight: The True Story of the Youngest Person to Climb the Seven Summits.* New York: Simon & Schuster Books for Young Readers, 2014.

SECONDARY SOURCES

Cohn, Jessica. *Mountain Climbing.* New York: Gareth Stevens Publishing, 2013.

Green, Sara. *Mountain Climbing.* Minneapolis: Bellwether Media, Inc., 2013.

Young, Jeff C. *Belaying the Line: Mountain, Rock, and Ice Climbing.* Edina, MN: ABDO Pub., 2011.

WEB SITES

American Alpine Club: https://www.americanalpineclub.org

American Mountain Guides Association: https://amga.com

International Climbing and Mountaineering Federation: http://www.theuiaa.org/

Glossary

altitude (AL-ti-tood) elevation above sea level

avalanches (AV-uh-lanch-iz) quick flows of snow down a slope

base camp (BASE KAMP) where climbers and helpers prepare for climbs and where tents, food, equipment, and medical supplies are stored

crampons (KRAM-ponz) mountain climbing gear that is attached to boots to clamp on to snow and ice

eight-thousanders (AYT THOU-zuhnd-urz) mountains that are over 8,000 meters (26,247 feet) tall

fluid (FLOO-id) liquid or water

ogre (OH-gur) monster

porters (POR-turz) people who carry other people's things

strenuous (STREN-yoo-uhs) really difficult

suffocate (SUHF-uh-kate) to die from being unable to breathe

summited (SUHM-it-id) reached the top

ultra marathons (UHL-truh MAR-uh-thahnz) footraces that are longer than a marathon (26 miles or 42 km)

Index

altitude, 14–16, 28, 30
Annapurna, 6

deaths, 4, 6, 7, 9, 25, 29
death zone, 15, 19

earthquake, 12, 24–25
eight-thousanders, 5, 6–7, 9, 12, 23
Everest, 7, 9, 10, 16, 21, 23, 24–25, 26, 28, 29

frostbite, 21, 26, 28

Himalayas, 5, 20, 30
Hood, Mount, 30

injuries, 15, 21, 25, 26, 28

K2, 4

lingo, 22

McKinley, Mount, 30
mountain climbing
- dangers, 15–19, 21, 24–28
- gear, 10–13
- lingo, 22
- making it extreme, 14–19
- records, 6–7, 9, 10, 23, 30
- who does it, 4–9
- women, 4–5, 7, 24–25, 30

Nepal, 12, 24

Ogre, The, 26
oxygen, 7, 9, 12, 14, 15, 16, 19, 20–23, 26

Pakistan, 26, 31
porters, 5, 9, 14, 20, 22

Seven Summits, 10–11, 31
Sherpas, 7, 30
summiting, 4

training, 16